FLASHES OF FIRE

66 DEVOTIONALS AND PRAYERS ACROSS SCRIPTURE

LEV MONTGOMERY

Copyright © 2025 by Pen & Press Publishing LLC. All rights reserved.

No part of this publication may be reproduced, stored in a retrieval system, or transmitted in any form or by any means—electronic, mechanical, photocopying, recording, or otherwise—without the prior written permission of the publisher, except in the case of brief quota-tions for the purpose of review or academic commentary.

Flashes of Fire is a publication of Pen & Press Publishing LLC | Pen & Press Holdings LLC.

All Scripture references are from the ESV unless otherwise noted. Published in the United States by: Pen & Press Publishing LLC

ISBN: 979-8-218-82515-7

Dedication

To my Lord and Savior, Jesus Christ— The Living Word and Consuming Fire.

To my family and faithful friends—Your prayers, support, and encouragement have been oxygen to this flame

"Is not my word like fire, declares the Lord, and like a hammer that breaks the rock in pieces?"

Jeremiah 23:29

Preface

Fire falls fast. It ignites, refines, and reveals. So does the Word.

This devotional volume offers sixty-six divine flashes—one from every book of Scripture. Each entry opens with a Scripture Spark—a catalytic verse drawn from the heart of the text. What follows is a Lightning Devotional—brief, vivid, and spirit-sharp—crafted to strike deep and burn long. Then, you're led into a Powerful Prayer, guided by five movements: Adoration, Confession, Petition, Declaration, and Amen.

To close each encounter, you'll receive a final ember—a one-line insight shaped by its biblical section:

- The First Light kindles the foundation.

- The Prophetic Fire tests and illumines the soul.

- The Eternal Flame reveals Christ and the birth of His Kingdom.

These are not lengthy meditations. They are strikes of holy fire—quick to consume the kindling of apathy, pride, fear, and unbelief.

Whether you read through in order or follow the Spirit's leading, may each devotional be a spark that sets your heart ablaze.

Welcome to the fire.

Lev Montgomery

Table Of Content

The First Light 14

Genesis 1:3 — "Light Be" 15
Exodus 14:14 – "Stand Still" 17
Leviticus 20:26 – "Set Apart" 19
Numbers 6:24-26 – "The Lord Bless You" 21
Deuteronomy 6:5 – "With All Your Heart" 23
Joshua 1:9 – "Do No Fear" 25
Judges 6:14 – "The Strength You Have" 27
Ruth 1:16 – "Covenant Love" 29
Samuel 17:45 – "In the Name of the Lord" 31
Samuel 22:31 – "Shield for Refuge" 33
Kings 18:37 – "Answer Me, O Lord" 35
Kings 6:16 – "Open Their Eyes" 37
Chronicles 16:11 – "Seek His Strength" 39
Chronicles 7:14 – "Heal the Land" 41
Ezra 7:10 – "Set His Heart" 43
Nehemiah 8:10 – "Strength Through Joy" 45
Esther 4:14 – "For This Moment" 47

The Prophetic Fire 49

Job 19:25 – "I Know My Redeemer" 50
Psalm 23:1 – "I Shall Not Want" 52
Proverbs 3:5-6 – "Straight Paths" 54
Ecclesiastes 3:11 – "In Its Time" 56
Song of Solomon 2:4 – "Banner Over Me" 58
Isaiah 40:31 – "They Shall Rise" 60
Jeremiah 29:11 – "Plans to Prosper" 62
Lamentations 3:22-23 – "Great Is Thy Faithfulness" 64
Ezekiel 36:26 – "Heart of Flesh" 66
Daniel 3:17-18 – "But If Not" 68
Hosea 6:1 – "He Will Revive" 70
Joel 2:28 – "I Will Pour Out" 72

Amos 5:24 – "Justice Like Waters" 74
Obadiah 1:15 – "As You Have Done" 76
Jonah 2:2 – "Out of the Belly" 78
Micah 6:8 – "What the Lord Requires" 80
Nahum 1:7 – "The Lord Is Good" 82
Habakkuk 3:17-18 – "Yet I Will Rejoice" 84
Zephaniah 3:17 – "Mighty to Save" 86
Haggai 2:9 – "Greater Glory Coming" 88
Zechariah 4:6 – "By My Spirit" 90
Malachi 4:2 – "Healing in His Wings" 92

The Eternal Flame 94

Matthew 11:28 – "Rest for Your Souls" 95
Mark 10:45 – "Ransom for Many" 97
Luke 15:20 – "While He Was Far Off" 99
Luke 24:32 – "Hearts Burned Within" 101
John 1:14 – "Full of Grace and Truth" 103
John 10:11 – "The Good Shepherd" 105
John 20:16 – "Mary" 107
John 21:17 – "Do You Love Me?" 109
Acts 1:8 – "Witnesses to the Ends" 111
Romans 8:28 – "All Things for Good" 113
1 Corinthians 1:27 – "Foolish to Shame the Wise" 115
2 Corinthians 12:9 – "Grace Is Sufficient" 117
Galatians 2:20 – "Christ Lives in Me" 119
Ephesians 3:20 – "More Than We Ask" 121
Philippians 1:6 – "He Will Complete It" 123
Colossians 1:17 – "Held Together" 125
1 Thessalonians 5:24 – "He Will Do It" 127
2 Thessalonians 3:3 – "The Lord Is Faithful" 129
1 Timothy 6:12 – "Fight the Good Fight" 131
2 Timothy 1:7 – "Spirit of Power" 133
Titus 3:5 – "Not by Works" 135
Philemon 1:6 – "Faith Becomes Effective" 137
Hebrews 4:12 – "Sharper Than a Sword" 139
James 1:5 – "Ask for Wisdom" 141

1 Peter 5:7 – "Cast Your Cares" 143
1 John 4:18 – "Perfect Love Casts Out Fear" 145
2 John 1:6 & 3 John 1:4 – "Walk in the Truth" 147
Revelation 21:5 – "All Things New" 149

Flashes of Fire:
66 Devotionals and Prayers
Across Scripture

By Lev Montgomery

"Is not my word like fire, declares the Lord, and like a hammer that breaks the rock in pieces?"

Acknowledgments

To the Pen & Press faithful —your hunger for holy beauty keeps the mission burning.

To every ministry supporter—thank you for carrying vision with prayer and provision.

To The Vanguard Circle—your spiritual precision, creative brilliance, and covenant loyalty have helped forge this fire. You are the sparks behind the pages.

Introduction

Scripture is not passive literature—it is living fire. It doesn't just inform; it ignites.

From Genesis to Revelation, the Word of God reveals a blazing narrative: the relentless pursuit of a holy God for His people, and the divine invitation to burn with His presence. These sixty-six devotionals are not casual reflections—they are summonses to encounter.

Each entry is intentionally brief but spiritually potent. You will not find long essays or exhaustive commentary here. Instead, you will find flashes of divine insight—crafted to cut through noise, awaken awe, and invite you into deeper communion with the Word Himself. We've structured this journey through three movements:

The First Light delivers the foundational force of the Law and History. The Prophetic Fire illuminates the cries of Wisdom and the fire of the Prophets.

The Eternal Flame draws you into Christ's voice, the Spirit's outpouring, and the glory of the New Creation.

This isn't just a read—it's a rhythm. A special cadence. A routine ritual for modern-day saints and seekers.

If you're holding this book, or reading this in digital form you likely sense it: the flicker of hunger, the subtle voice of calling, the urgency of fire.

Let every verse strike. Let every prayer rise. Let every spark become flame. This is your invitation. Not to study the fire. But to step into it.

Lev Montgomery

The First Light

Genesis 1:3
"Light Be"

The Spark
"And God said, 'Let there be light,' and there was light."

The Devotional
Creation began not with motion, but with a voice. The cosmos was not birthed through chaos clawing its way into order, but by the decree of the Living God. One sentence split eternity from emptiness: "Light be."

Darkness did not resist. It simply fled.

This first flash of divine speech is the template for all transformation. God speaks, and what He speaks becomes. When His Word goes forth, it cannot return void. Light is not a suggestion—it is a command, an unchallengeable verdict against the reign of shadows.

And the same voice that spoke galaxies into existence still speaks into your life. Over the voids of confusion, the chaos of anxiety, the darkness of sin—His decree is the same: "Light be."

Will you let His Word confront your shadows? Will you allow the divine decree to scatter the night you've grown accustomed to?

The God who ignited suns still speaks. And when He speaks, light must come.

The Prayer

Adoration: Lord, You are Light, eternal and uncreated, in whom there is no shadow at all. Confession: Forgive me for tolerating darkness—compromise, fear, and unbelief. Petition: Speak again over my heart, Lord. Order my chaos, scatter the shadows, and kindle my faith. Declaration: I declare that where Your Word goes forth, light will shine, and no darkness can overcome it. Amen.

Ember Reflection (The First Light)
"Every dawn begins with a word."

The Charge

Carry His Word into today. Speak light where you see despair. Prophesy dawn where others see only night.

Exodus 14:14
"Stand Still"

The Spark
"The Lord will fight for you; you have only to be silent."

The Devotional
Israel stood trapped between the Red Sea and Pharaoh's army. Terror surged. Logic demanded panic, but God demanded trust. His word was not a battle plan, but a posture: stand still.

This is the scandal of faith. When strength fails, silence becomes the strategy. God Himself wages war, and His arm is never shortened. The stillness He commands is not passivity but surrender—a refusal to let fear dictate the next move.

In your life, the armies may roar and the waters may rise. The command remains the same: stand still. God does not ask for frantic effort but for unshaken trust.

His fight is your victory.

The Prayer
Adoration: Lord, You are my Defender, strong and mighty in battle. Confession: Forgive me for rushing ahead in fear, grasping for control. Petition: Teach me to be still when You are moving.

Declaration: I declare that no enemy can withstand the One who fights for me. Amen.

The Reflection (The First Light)
"Stillness is strength when God is near."

The Charge
Today, resist the urge to strive. Let God's fight be your peace.

Leviticus 20:26
"Set Apart"

The Spark
"You shall be holy to me, for I the Lord am holy and have separated you from the peoples, that you should be mine."

The Devotional
Holiness is not primarily about rules; it is about belonging. God's call to His people was not simply to behave differently, but to be His possession—set apart for His glory.

Holiness is costly, because it demands separation from what is common. To belong to God is to be marked, to live as one who reflects His nature. This separation is not punishment, but privilege. The Holy One draws near and claims His people as His own.

In Christ, this calling remains. You are not your own. You were bought with a price. Holiness is not a burden—it is the highest honor: to bear the name of the Lord and reflect His light in a world of shadows.

The Prayer
Adoration: Holy God, You alone are perfect, pure, and glorious. Confession: Forgive me for blurring the line between sacred and profane. Petition: Set me apart, Lord—shape me to reflect Your holiness. Declaration: I declare that I am Yours, consecrated to Your glory. Amen.

The Reflection (The First Light)
"To be holy is to belong."

The Charge
Walk today as one marked by God. Let His holiness shine through your choices.

Numbers 6:24-26
"The Lord Bless You"

The Spark
"The Lord bless you and keep you; the Lord make his face to shine upon you and be gracious to you; the Lord lift up his countenance upon you and give you peace.

The Devotional
This priestly blessing is more than a benediction—it is God's own desire spoken over His people. Notice the rhythm: blessing, protection, favor, peace. Every line draws the worshiper deeper into the warmth of God's face.

To live under this blessing is to live under God's gaze—not as one condemned, but as one cherished. His countenance does not merely glance; it rests. His peace is not a fragile truce but a wholeness no enemy can shatter.

In Christ, this blessing is sealed. We are kept, graced, and lifted by the High Priest who intercedes forever. The words Moses spoke are words Jesus fulfills.

The Prayer Adoration
Lord, Your face is light and life. Confession: Forgive me for seeking blessing apart from You. Petition: Shine Your favor upon me, Lord, and guard my steps. Declaration: I declare that Your peace is greater than my turmoil. Amen.

The Reflection (The First Light)
"The greatest gift is God's gaze."

The Charge
Walk today as one kept by the Lord's blessing.

Deuteronomy 6:5
"With All Your Heart"

The Spark
"You shall love the Lord your God with all your heart and with all your soul and with all your might."

The Devotional
The greatest command is not complicated—it is consuming. God does not ask for part of the heart but all of it. Love is not measured in fragments but in fullness.

This verse dismantles half-hearted faith. It refuses casual devotion. It summons the whole self—affections, thoughts, strength—into total surrender.

Such love is only possible because He first loved us. The God who commands love also empowers it. He fills what He requires, igniting hearts that would otherwise grow cold.

The Prayer
Adoration: Lord, You are worthy of my whole life. Confession: Forgive me for offering divided love. Petition: Enlarge my heart to burn for You alone.

Declaration: I declare that my soul, mind, and strength belong to You. Amen.

The Reflection   (The First Light)
"Love is full when it is all."

The Charge
Today, love Him without reserve.

Joshua 1:9
"Do No Fear"

The Spark
"Have I not commanded you? Be strong and courageous. Do not be frightened, and do not be dismayed, for the Lord your God is with you wherever you go."

The Devotional
God does not comfort Joshua with easy circumstances but with His presence. Strength and courage are not emotions to summon but gifts rooted in God's nearness.

Fear thrives in imagined absence. Courage thrives in remembered presence. Wherever the call of God leads, He goes too. The courage to step forward is born not in ourselves but in the certainty that He is with us.

The Prayer
Adoration: Lord, You are my strong tower. Confession: Forgive me for letting fear dictate my steps. Petition: Fill me with Your courage to obey fully.
Declaration: I declare that You are with me wherever I go. Amen.

The Reflection (The First Light)
"Courage is presence remembered."

The Charge
Step forward today knowing He goes with you.

Judges 6:14
"The Strength You Have"

The Spark
"Go in the strength you have and save Israel out of Midian's hand. Am I not sending you?"

The Devotional
We often delay obedience, waiting to feel "ready." But God's call is not based on our confidence; it is anchored in His authority. The question is not, "Am I strong enough?" but "Has He sent me?" If He has, then His strength will be revaled in our weakness.

The Prayer
Adoration: Lord, You are my strength and my song. Confession: Forgive me for hiding in fear and doubting Your call. Petition: Teach me to trust Your sending more than my weakness. Declaration: I declare that Your presence makes me strong. Amen.

The Reflection   (The First Light)
"God calls, then qualifies."

The Charge
Go forward today in the strength you have—He will provide the rest.

Ruth 1:16
"Covenant Love"

The Spark
"Where you go I will go, and where you lodge I will lodge. Your people shall be my people, and your God my God."

The Devotional
Ruth's words to Naomi are more than loyalty—they are covenant. She forsook her homeland, security, and familiar gods to bind herself to Naomi's God and people.

This love foreshadows Christ's love for His Church, and the Church's love for Him. It is love that clings, not casually but covenantally. True faith is not convenience—it is costly commitment. Ruth's devotion led her into God's redemptive story, and through her, the Messiah's line was carried forward.

The Prayer
Adoration: Lord, You are the faithful Covenant-Keeper. Confession: Forgive me for treating commitment lightly. Petition: Root me in love that clings even when it costs. Declaration: I declare that Your covenant love holds me fast. Amen.

The Reflection   (The First Light)
"Covenant love writes redemptive history."

The Charge
Choose covenant love today—cling to God and those He has given you.

Samuel 17:45
"In the Name of the Lord"

The Spark
"You come to me with a sword and with a spear and with a javelin, but I come to you in the name of the Lord of hosts."

The Devotional
David faced Goliath without conventional weapons. His confidence was not in sword or armor but in the name of the Lord. The battle was not size against size, but God against defiance.

When we face giants—obstacles, fears, sins—our victory is not in our skill but in His name. To invoke His name is not superstition but covenant identity. His reputation, His authority, His power stand behind His people.

The Prayer
Adoration: Lord, You are the Lord of hosts, the God who fights for me. Confession: Forgive me for trusting in human weapons over Your name. Petition: Teach me to face every giant with faith in You. Declaration: I declare that every battle belongs to the Lord. Amen.

The Reflection   (The First Light)
"Victory rests in His name, not our weapons."

The Charge
Face today's giants in His authority, not your own.

Samuel 22:31
"Shield for Refuge"

The Spark
"This God—his way is perfect; the word of the Lord proves true; he is a shield for all those who take refuge in him."

The Devotional
David declares God's word flawless and His protection unfailing. To trust Him is to enter a fortress stronger than any enemy.

God does not promise the absence of arrows but the presence of a shield. His word proves true not in theory but in trial. Every refuge apart from Him eventually fails; He alone is unbreakable.

The Prayer
Adoration: Lord, You are my perfect refuge. Confession: Forgive me for seeking shelter in what cannot save. Petition: Hide me under the shadow of Your shield. Declaration: I declare that Your word stands true in every battle. Amen.

The Reflection   (The First Light)
"His word proves true in the fire."

The Charge
Take refuge in Him today—His shield never fails.

Kings 18:37
"Answer Me, O Lord"

The Spark
"Answer me, O Lord, answer me, that this people may know that you, O Lord, are God, and that you have turned their hearts back."

The Devotional
Elijah's prayer on Mount Carmel was not a display of his power but a plea for God's glory. Fire fell, not to prove Elijah, but to reveal God and call His people back.

True prayer seeks God's vindication, not our own. It burns with the desire that all may see He alone is Lord. Revival is not about spectacle but about hearts turned back to Him.

The Prayer
Adoration: Lord, You alone are God. Confession: Forgive me for praying to be seen rather than to see You revealed. Petition: Turn hearts back to You in my generation. Declaration: I declare that You answer prayer to magnify Your name. Amen.

The Reflection (The First Light)
"Prayer is fire when it seeks His glory."

The Charge
Pray today for God's name to be exalted, not your own.

Kings 6:16
"Open Their Eyes"

The Spark
"Do not be afraid, for those who are with us are more than those who are with them."

The Devotional
Elisha's servant trembled at the sight of an enemy army. But Elisha saw deeper— the hills were ablaze with horses and chariots of fire. The servant's fear was not rooted in reality but blindness.

Faith sees what eyes cannot. The unseen is greater than the seen. God's armies surround His people still. The question is not, "Are we outnumbered?" but "Will we see?"

The Prayer
Adoration: Lord, You are the Lord of hosts, and heaven's armies obey You. Confession: Forgive me for fearing what I can see more than trusting what is unseen. Petition: Open my eyes to the reality of Your presence and power.

Declaration: I declare that greater are those with us than against us. Amen.

The Reflection (The First Light)
"Faith sees the unseen."

The Charge
Ask God to open your eyes today—His armies still surround you.

Chronicles 16:11
"Seek His Strength"

The Spark
"Seek the Lord and his strength; seek his presence continually!"

The Devotional
David's psalm is a summons to unceasing pursuit. God does not invite occasional glances but continual seeking. His strength is inexhaustible, and His presence is the true prize.

To seek Him continually is to live awake to His nearness in every moment— ordinary or extraordinary. Strength is not found in self-effort but in communion. The more we seek, the more we discover that He was already seeking us.

The Prayer
Adoration: Lord, You are my strength and my portion forever. Confession: Forgive me for seeking substitutes instead of Your presence. Petition: Draw me into continual communion with You. Declaration: I declare that Your presence is my strength. Amen.

The Reflection (The First Light)
"Strength is sustained by presence."

The Charge
Turn your heart toward Him often today—He will meet you there.

Chronicles 7:14
"Heal the Land"

The Spark
"If my people who are called by my name humble themselves, and pray and seek my face and turn from their wicked ways, then I will hear from heaven and will forgive their sin and heal their land."

The Devotional
God ties national restoration to spiritual repentance. The healing of the land begins not in politics but in prayer. Revival flows from humility, repentance, and seeking His face.

We cannot expect transformation around us without transformation within us. God hears the cry of a humbled people, and His forgiveness is always the first step toward healing.

The Prayer
Adoration: Lord, You are merciful and mighty to forgive. Confession: Forgive our sins and heal our waywardness. Petition: Turn our hearts back to You; bring revival to our land. Declaration: I declare that You hear and forgive when Your people repent. Amen.

The Reflection (The First Light)
"National healing begins with humble hearts."

The Charge
Pray today for forgiveness and healing in your community and nation.

Ezra 7:10
"Set His Heart"

The Spark
"For Ezra had set his heart to study the Law of the Lord, and to do it and to teach his statutes and rules in Israel."

The Devotional
Ezra's ministry was rooted in a threefold devotion: study, obedience, and teaching. He did not simply accumulate knowledge—he practiced it, and then passed it on. His heart was set, immovable in focus.

Spiritual influence begins in the secret place, is proven in obedience, and flows into teaching. We cannot lead others where we have not first gone ourselves.

The Prayer
Adoration: Lord, You are the giver of wisdom and truth. Confession: Forgive me for knowing without doing. Petition: Set my heart firmly to learn, obey, and teach Your word. Declaration: I declare that my heart belongs to Your Word. Amen.

The Reflection (The First Light)
"True authority is learned, lived, and then taught."

The Charge
Set your heart on God's Word today—let it shape both your life and your witness.

Nehemiah 8:10
"Strength Through Joy"

The Spark
"Do not be grieved, for the joy of the Lord is your strength."

The Devotional
As God's Word was read, the people wept under conviction. Yet Nehemiah redirected them toward celebration. Their grief was real, but God's grace was greater. Joy became their strength, not sorrow.

The joy of the Lord is not shallow happiness but deep assurance that God is faithful. Joy is not the denial of hardship—it is the declaration that God is greater than hardship. Strength rises when joy takes root.

The Prayer
Adoration: Lord, You are my exceeding joy. Confession: Forgive me for letting sorrow define me. Petition: Restore to me the joy of Your salvation. Declaration: I declare that Your joy is my strength. Amen.

The Reflection   (The First Light)
"Strength is born from holy joy."

The Charge
Rejoice in the Lord today—let His joy be your strength.

Esther 4:14
"For This Moment"

The Spark
"And who knows whether you have not come to the kingdom for such a time as this?"

The Devotional
Mordecai's words to Esther pierce with destiny. Her position was not random but providential. The moment of crisis revealed her calling.

God places His people in specific times and places for purposes greater than themselves. Courage is required, but it is courage born of conviction that God writes history through willing vessels. To remain silent is to risk irrelevance; to act in faith is to step into destiny.

The Prayer
Adoration: Lord, You are sovereign over times and seasons. Confession: Forgive me for shrinking back from the moments You give. Petition: Grant me courage to act when my moment comes. Declaration: I declare that I was born for this time and this call. Amen.

The Reflection (The First Light)
"God ordains moments that demand courage."

The Charge
Embrace your moment today—step boldly into the place God has positioned you.

The Prophetic Fire

Job 19:25
"I Know My Redeemer"

The Spark
"For I know that my Redeemer lives, and at the last he will stand upon the earth."

The Devotional
Job sat in ashes, stripped of comfort, yet his confession pierced through despair. He staked his hope not on explanations but on a living Redeemer who would stand in final vindication.

Faith is never proven in ease but in fire. Job did not know how God would redeem, but he knew who God was. His confidence rested not in outcomes but in a Redeemer who lives beyond the grave.

In Christ, Job's longing finds fulfillment. Our Redeemer lives, and He will stand again on the earth—not in theory but in glory.

The Prayer
Adoration: Lord, You are my living Redeemer. Confession: Forgive me for doubting when suffering blinds me. Petition: Anchor me in hope beyond circumstances. Declaration: I declare that my Redeemer lives, and He will stand. Amen.

The Reflection (The Prophetic Fire)
"Hope is forged on the certainty of a living Redeemer."

The Charge
Cling to Christ today—your Redeemer is alive.

Psalm 23:1
"I Shall Not Want"

The Spark
"The Lord is my shepherd; I shall not want."

The Devotional
David begins not with circumstance but with identity: the Lord is Shepherd. Provision flows from His care, not our striving. To say, "I shall not want" is not denial of need but declaration of trust.

Sheep lack strategy, strength, or survival skills without the shepherd. But under His hand, lack is displaced by sufficiency. The Shepherd leads, restores, and guards—even in valleys of death. Christ, the Good Shepherd, secures this promise with His life.

The Prayer
Adoration: Lord, You are my Shepherd, my keeper, my guide. Confession: Forgive me for grasping as if I were alone. Petition: Lead me beside still waters today. Declaration: I declare that I shall not want, for You are enough. Amen.

The Reflection   (The Prophetic Fire)
"Want flees where the Shepherd leads."

The Charge
Rest in His provision—He is enough.

Proverbs 3:5-6
"Straight Paths"

The Spark
"Trust in the Lord with all your heart, and do not lean on your own understanding. In all your ways acknowledge him, and he will make straight your paths."

The Devotional
Wisdom begins with trust. Our own understanding bends, falters, and misleads, but God's wisdom cuts straight through confusion. Trust is not partial—it is wholehearted surrender.

To acknowledge Him in all our ways is to refuse self-sufficiency and invite His counsel into every decision. Straight paths are not easy paths, but they are sure. His guidance is not abstract but practical, meeting us in the steps we take daily.

The Prayer
Adoration: Lord, You are wisdom itself. Confession: Forgive me for leaning on my own understanding. Petition: Direct my steps today with Your clarity.

Declaration: I declare that my paths are straight because I trust You. Amen.

The Reflection   (The Prophetic Fire)
"Trust writes the map, obedience walks the path"

The Charge
Surrender your decisions to Him today—He will make the path straight.

Ecclesiastes 3:11
"In Its Time"

The Spark
"He has made everything beautiful in its time. Also, he has put eternity into man's heart, yet so that he cannot find out what God has done from the beginning to the end."

The Devotional
Time frustrates us because we long for eternity. God's work is beautiful, but His timing is His own. We see fragments; He sees the whole.

Faith rests not in knowing the schedule but in trusting the Artist. The eternal God writes beauty into seasons, even when we cannot perceive it. Eternity in our hearts whispers that we were made for more than this fleeting world, yet we bow to His timing, confident His design is perfect.

The Prayer
Adoration: Lord, You are the Lord of time and eternity. Confession: Forgive me for resenting Your timing. Petition: Teach me to trust Your seasons. Declaration: I declare that everything is made beautiful in its time. Amen.

The Reflection (The Prophetic Fire)
"Beauty unfolds in God's time, not ours."

The Charge
Rest in His timing today—eternity is already in your heart.

Song of Solomon 2:4 "Banner Over Me"

The Spark
"He brought me to the banqueting house, and his banner over me was love."

The Devotional
Love is not whispered in secrecy but displayed openly like a banner. In this image of covenant love, intimacy is celebrated, not hiden.God's banner over His people is not shame but steadfas love.

In Christ, the ultimate banner was lifted on the cross, declaring forever: "Loved." His love is not fragile affection but covenantal commitment. It covers, secures, and proclaims us His own.

The Prayer
Adoration: Lord, Your love is my covering and my song. Confession: Forgive me for doubting Your banner over my life. Petition: Wrap me in Your covenant love afresh today. Declaration: I declare that Your banner over me is love. Amen.

The Reflection (The Prophetic Fire)
"Love is the banner God raises over His own."

The Charge
Walk today as one marked by His unfailing love.

Isaiah 40:31
"They Shall Rise"

The Spark
"But they who wait for the Lord shall renew their strength; they shall mount up with wings like eagles; they shall run and not be weary; they shall walk and not faint."

The Devotional
Strength is not found in constant striving but in waiting—active trust in God's timing and presence. Those who wait are not idle; they are anchored. Their strength is renewed, not drained.

Isaiah gives three images: soaring, running, walking. God meets us in all seasons—moments of flight, endurance, and daily steps. In every pace, His renewal sustains us.

To wait on Him is to rise above exhaustion and live in the current of His Spirit.

The Prayer
Adoration: Lord, You are my strength and sustainer. Confession: Forgive me for rushing ahead in my own power. Petition: Teach me to wait well and renew me as I do. Declaration: I declare that I will rise, run, and walk in Your strength. Amen.

The Reflection (The Prophetic Fire)
"Waiting births renewal; trust gives wings."

The Charge
Wait on Him today; strength will rise where striving ends.

Jeremiah 29:11
"Plans to Prosper"

The Spark
"For I know the plans I have for you, declares the Lord, plans for welfare and not for evil, to give you a future and a hope."

The Devotional
Spoken to exiles in Babylon, this promise was not an escape hatch but a reassurance: God had not abandoned them. His plans were sovereign even in exile.

Hope is not the denial of hardship but the certainty that God writes the ending. His plans prosper not by avoiding trial but by redeeming it. Our future is not fragile—it is held in His hands.

The Prayer
Adoration: Lord, You are the Author of my future. Confession: Forgive me for doubting Your goodness when life is hard. Petition: Anchor me in Your hope when circumstances feel exiled. Declaration: I declare that Your plans for me are good and secure. Amen.

The Reflection (The Prophetic Fire)
"Exile cannot erase His plans."

The Charge
Trust His design today—your future rests in Him.

Lamentations 3:22-23 "Great Is Thy Faithfulness"

The Spark
"The steadfast love of the Lord never ceases; his mercies never come to an end; they are new every morning; great is your faithfulness."

The Devotional
Jeremiah wept over Jerusalem's ruins, yet from the ashes rose this confession: God's love does not end. His mercies are not rationed but renewed each morning.

The ruins remind us of sin's cost, but the sunrise reminds us of mercy's persistence. God's faithfulness is not seasonal—it is unbroken, even in lament. The darkest night cannot cancel the dawn.

The Prayer
Adoration: Lord, Your mercies are new every morning. Confession: Forgive me for forgetting Your faithfulness in sorrow. Petition: Teach me to trust Your mercies when ruins surround me. Declaration: I declare that Your love never ceases and Your faithfulness endures. Amen.

The Reflection (The Prophetic Fire)
"Mercy meets every morning."

The Charge
Rise today knowing His mercy is already waiting.

Ezekiel 36:26
"Heart of Flesh"

The Spark
"And I will give you a new heart, and a new spirit I will put within you. And I will remove the heart of stone from your flesh and give you a heart of flesh."

The Devotional
God's promise through Ezekiel is radical transformation. Religion reforms behavior, but God replaces hearts. A heart of stone—cold, unresponsive—is exchanged for a heart of flesh—living, tender, responsive to Him.

This is the essence of new covenant life: God Himself does the work. He gives what He commands. In Christ, hearts of stone are shattered, and by the Spirit, hearts of flesh are awakened.

The Prayer
Adoration: Lord, You are the giver of new hearts and new life. Confession: Forgive me for hardening my heart against You. Petition: Replace my stony heart with one alive to Your Spirit. Declaration: I declare that my heart beats with new life in You. Amen.

The Reflection   (The Prophetic Fire)
"Grace does not polish stone; it gives flesh."

The Charge
Ask Him today to keep your heart soft and alive to His voice.

Daniel 3:17-18
"But If Not"

The Spark
"If this be so, our God whom we serve is able to deliver us from the burning fiery furnace, and he will deliver us out of your hand, O king. But if not, be it known to you, O king, that we will not serve your gods or worship the golden image that you have set up."

The Devotional
Shadrach, Meshach, and Abednego's faith was not conditional. They knew God could deliver, but their loyalty did not depend on it. Even in the face of fire, their devotion was steadfast: "But if not, we will not bow."

True faith does not bargain with God. It clings to Him whether He rescues or not. Deliverance is His to choose; worship is ours to give. This is the fire-tested faith that overcomes compromise.

The Prayer
Adoration: Lord, You are worthy of worship, whether in fire or freedom. Confession: Forgive me for tying my worship to outcomes. Petition: Strengthen me to remain faithful in every furnace. Declaration: I declare that even if He does not, still I will not bow. Amen

The Reflection (The Prophetic Fire)
"Faith remains when outcomes do not."

The Charge
Stand today in unwavering devotion—whether He delivers or not, do not bow.

Hosea 6:1
"He Will Revive"

The Spark
"Come, let us return to the Lord; for he has torn us, that he may heal us; he has struck us down, and he will bind us up."

The Devotional
Hosea calls Israel to repentance with confidence in God's mercy. Though discipline wounded, His intent was never destruction but restoration. God tears to heal, strikes to bind, wounds to revive.

Repentance is not groveling before a cruel master—it is running into the arms of a healer. The One who disciplines is the same One who restores. His judgments are surgical; His aim is always revival.

The Prayer
Adoration: Lord, You are healer of the broken and restorer of the fallen. Confession: Forgive me for resisting Your discipline. Petition: Revive me as I return to You. Declaration: I declare that where You wound, You also heal. Amen.

The Reflection   (The Prophetic Fire)
"His wounds are for healing; His strikes for revival."

The Charge
Return to Him today—His arms are open, His healing sure.

Joel 2:28
"I Will Pour Out"

The Spark
"And it shall come to pass afterward, that I will pour out my Spirit on all flesh; your sons and your daughters shall prophesy, your old men shall dream dreams, and your young men shall see visions."

The Devotional
The Spirit is not given for private comfort but public witness. Prophecy, dreams, and visions mark a people saturated with His presence. This is God's promise: not a trickle, but a flood.

The Prayer
Adoration: Lord, You are the giver of the Spirit without measure. Confession: Forgive me for living as if the Spirit's power is scarce. Petition: Pour Your Spirit on me afresh today. Declaration: I declare that Your promise is for all flesh, including me. Amen.

The Reflection (The Prophetic Fire)
"The Spirit is not rationed—He is poured."

The Charge
Ask boldly for His Spirit today—and expect overflow.

Amos 5:24
"Justice Like Waters"

The Spark
"But let justice roll down like waters, and righteousness like an ever-flowing stream."

The Devotional
Amos rebuked empty religion—songs without obedience, offerings without justice. God desires not ritual performance but righteousness embodied. Justice is not optional; it is the outflow of knowing Him

Waters roll, streams flow. Justice and righteousness are not stagnant but moving—continuous, unstoppable, cleansing. A worshiping people must be a just people. Anything less is noise to His ears.

The Prayer
Adoration: Lord, You are righteous and just in all Your ways. Confession: Forgive me for honoring You with lips while neglecting justice. Petition: Let righteousness flow through my life and community. Declaration: I declare that Your justice will roll like mighty waters. Amen.

The Reflection   (The Prophetic Fire)
"True worship flows as justice and righteousness."

The Charge
Live today as a stream of righteousness, not a stagnant pool.

Obadiah 1:15
"As You Have Done"

The Spark
"For the day of the Lord is near upon all the nations. As you have done, it shall be done to you; your deeds shall return on your own head."

The Devotional
Obadiah's brief prophecy confronts Edom's pride and cruelty. The principle is clear: the day of the Lord brings justice, and deeds return upon the doer. God's justice is not partial—nations and individuals alike reap what they sow.

For the believer, this warning is also a call to humility and mercy. In Christ, justice and mercy meet—our judgment fell on Him, and His righteousness is given to us. But the principle remains: pride leads to downfall, and cruelty rebounds.

The Prayer
Adoration: Lord, You are the righteous Judge of all nations. Confession: Forgive me for pride and for sowing what dishonors You. Petition: Teach me to sow mercy, justice, and humility. Declaration: I declare that what I sow in Christ will reap eternal life. Amen.

The Reflection (The Prophetic Fire)
"The day of the Lord brings every deed to light."

The Charge
Sow today what you will rejoice to reap tomorrow.

Jonah 2:2
"Out of the Belly"

The Spark
"I called out to the Lord, out of my distress, and he answered me; out of the belly of Sheol I cried, and you heard my voice."

The Devotional
Jonah prayed from the depths—literally swallowed by the sea and figuratively swallowed by disobedience. Yet from that place of despair, God heard.

No pit is too deep, no rebellion too strong to silence His mercy. Jonah's cry from the belly of the fish became the turning point. God answers even when we are there by our own fault.

Christ Himself echoed Jonah's descent, entering the grave for our sake—and rising in victory. Our cries in the depths are not ignored; they are heard by the God who redeems.

The Prayer
Adoration: Lord, You hear from the depths. Confession: Forgive me for running from Your call. Petition: Rescue me from the depths of my own rebellion.

Declaration: I declare that even in the belly of despair, You answer. Amen.

The Reflection (The Prophetic Fire)
"No depth silences His mercy."

The Charge
Cry out today, no matter how far you've run—He hears.

Micah 6:8
"What the Lord Requires"

The Spark
"He has told you, O man, what is good; and what does the Lord require of you but to do justice, and to love kindness, and to walk humbly with your God?"

The Devotional
Micah distills religion to its essence. God does not crave ritual without righteousness. What He requires is not hidden—it is clear: justice, kindness, humility.

Justice without love becomes harsh. Love without justice becomes hollow. Humility anchors both, keeping us aligned with His character. This is worship that pleases Him—not sacrifice of bulls, but a life reflecting His heart.

The Prayer
Adoration: Lord, You are just, kind, and humble in majesty. Confession: Forgive me for substituting rituals for righteousness. Petition: Shape my heart to reflect Your justice, mercy, and humility. Declaration: I declare that I will walk humbly with my God. Amen.

The Reflection   (The Prophetic Fire)
"What He requires is what He empowers."

The Charge
Live today in justice, kindness, and humility—this is true worship.

Nahum 1:7
"The Lord Is Good"

The Spark
"The Lord is good, a stronghold in the day of trouble; he knows those who take refuge in him."

The Devotional
Amid judgment pronounced on Nineveh, Nahum reminds God's people of His goodness. He is both Judge and Refuge. His goodness is not negated by wrath; it shines in His protection of those who trust Him.

In days of trouble, God is not distant—He is stronghold. His goodness is not abstract but personal: "He knows those who take refuge in him." To be known by Him is safety beyond circumstance.

The Prayer
Adoration: Lord, You are good, and Your mercy endures forever. Confession: Forgive me for doubting Your goodness in hardship. Petition: Be my stronghold in the day of trouble. Declaration: I declare that the Lord is my refuge and knows me by name. Amen.

The Reflection   (The Prophetic Fire)
"Goodness is strongest in trouble."

The Charge
Run into His stronghold today—He knows you.

Habakkuk 3:17-18
"Yet" I Will Rejoice"

The Spark
"Though the fig tree should not blossom, nor fruit be on the vines... yet I will rejoice in the Lord; I will take joy in the God of my salvation."

The Devotional
Habakkuk envisions total collapse—no crops, no flocks, no livelihood. Yet his resolve is stunning: "Yet I will rejoice." Joy is not rooted in circumstances but in God Himself.

This is the defiance of faith: to worship in scarcity, to rejoice when all else is stripped away. Salvation is secure even when sustenance is gone. Joy in God is stronger than loss.

The Prayer
Adoration: Lord, You are my salvation and my joy. Confession: Forgive me for tying joy to abundance. Petition: Teach me to rejoice in You regardless of circumstance. Declaration: I declare that my joy is rooted in the unchanging God. Amen.

The Reflection (The Prophetic Fire)
"Joy rooted in God outlasts loss."

The Charge
Choose joy today—even in lack, rejoice in Him.

Zephaniah 3:17 "Mighty to Save"

The Spark
"The Lord your God is in your midst, a mighty one who will save; he will rejoice over you with gladness; he will quiet you by his love; he will exult over you with loud singing."

The Devotional
Zephaniah reveals God not only as mighty Savior but as rejoicing Father. He is in the midst of His people—not distant, but present. He saves with power, loves with gentleness, and sings with delight.

To be quieted by His love is to rest in a security deeper than fear. To be sung over by God is to know joy beyond measure. Salvation is not just rescue—it is relationship.

The Prayer
Adoration: Lord, You are mighty to save and tender in love. Confession: Forgive me for doubting Your delight in me. Petition: Quiet my soul with Your love today. Declaration: I declare that the Lord rejoices over me with singing. Amen.

The Reflection (The Prophetic Fire)
"He saves with power and sings with joy."

The Charge
Rest today in His love—He rejoices over you.

Haggai 2:9
"Greater Glory Coming"

The Spark
"The latter glory of this house shall be greater than the former, says the Lord of hosts. And in this place I will give peace."

The Devotional
The temple rebuilt after exile seemed small, unimpressive. Yet God promised a future glory greater than the past. The measure of His house is not in stone but in His presence.

This promise points to Christ, the true Temple, and to the Spirit dwelling in His Church. The greater glory is not architecture but incarnation. And the peace He gives surpasses all the former splendor.

The Prayer
Adoration: Lord, You are the glory of Your house. Confession: Forgive me for measuring by sight instead of promise. Petition: Fill Your Church with greater glory. Declaration: I declare that the glory to come is greater than the former. Amen.

The Reflection (The Prophetic Fire)
"Greater glory is presence, not stone."

The Charge
Look beyond appearances today—the greater glory is coming.

Zechariah 4:6
"By My Spirit"

The Spark
"Not by might, nor by power, but by my Spirit, says the Lord of hosts."

The Devotional
God reminded Zerubbabel that rebuilding the temple would not depend on human effort but divine Spirit. Strength and strategies, though useful, cannot accomplish what only the Spirit can.

Our lives, too, are not advanced by sheer force but by the Spirit's breath. Might and power exhaust; His Spirit empowers. What God begins in the Spirit must be finished by the Spirit.

The Prayer
Adoration: Lord, You are the Spirit who empowers and sustains. Confession: Forgive me for relying on my own strength. Petition: Fill me afresh with Your Spirit's power. Declaration: I declare that by His Spirit, the work will be done. Amen.

The Reflection (The Prophetic Fire)
"The Spirit accomplishes what strength cannot."

The Charge
Lean not on your power today—move by His Spirit.

Malachi 4:2
"Healing in His Wings"

The Spark
"But for you who fear my name, the sun of righteousness shall rise with healing in its wings. You shall go out leaping like calves from the stall."

The Devotional
Malachi closes with promise: judgment for the arrogant, but healing for those who fear His name. The image is of the rising sun, spreading warmth and restoration.

This points to Christ, the Sun of Righteousness, whose appearing brings healing to the broken and freedom to the bound. In Him, dawn has come, and with it, wholeness.

The Prayer
Adoration: Lord, You are the Sun of Righteousness, my healer and restorer. Confession: Forgive me for lingering in shadows. Petition: Shine Your healing light into every wounded place. Declaration: I declare that healing rises with Christ my Lord. Amen.

The Reflection   (The Prophetic Fire)
"Christ rises with healing in His light."

The Charge
Step into His light today—healing is found in Him.

The Eternal Flame

Matthew 11:28
"Rest for Your Souls"

The Spark
"Come to me, all who labor and are heavy laden, and I will give you rest."

The Devotional
Christ does not invite the strong but the weary. His rest is not escape but exchange: burdens lifted, yokes made light by His presence. True rest is found not in a place but a Person.

We carry burdens He never asked us to bear. At His feet, the restless find quiet, the heavy find ease. The soul's rest is not in finished tasks but in a finished cross.

The Prayer
Adoration: Lord, You are rest for the weary and peace for the burdened. Confession: Forgive me for carrying what You call me to lay down. Petition: Teach me to rest in You, not in my own strength. Declaration: I declare that my soul rests secure in Christ. Amen.

The Reflection   (The Eternal Flame)
"Rest is found in a Person, not a place."

The Charge
Lay down your burdens today—He offers rest.

Mark 10:45
"Ransom for Many"

The Spark
"For even the Son of Man came not to be served but to serve, and to give his life as a ransom for many."

The Devotional
Greatness in the kingdom is inverted. The King stooped to serve, the Lord laid down His life. His ransom was the price of freedom, paid not with silver but with blood.

Service is not beneath the Son of Man, nor beneath His followers. True leadership is sacrifice; true power is poured out for others. To follow Him is to embrace the cross-shaped path of servanthood.

The Prayer
Adoration: Lord, You are the Servant King who gave Your life for me. Confession: Forgive me for seeking to be served rather than to serve. Petition: Make me more like You in humility and sacrifice. Declaration: I declare that I am ransomed and free in Christ. Amen.

The Reflection (The Eternal Flame)
"Greatness stoops to serve."

The Charge
Serve someone today in the spirit of Christ your King.

Luke 15:20
"While He Was Far Off"

The Spark
"But while he was still a long way off, his father saw him and felt compassion, and ran and embraced him and kissed him."

The Devotional
The prodigal rehearsed shame; the father rehearsed compassion. Before confession was spoken, embrace was given. The Father runs, not reluctantly but eagerly, to welcome home.

This is the heart of God: mercy in motion, love that anticipates repentance with embrace. Our return is never met with cold tolerance but with overwhelming joy.

The Prayer
Adoration: Lord, You are the Father who runs to meet the lost. Confession: Forgive me for believing You would reject me. Petition: Let me rest in Your embrace today. Declaration: I declare that I am welcomed and loved in Christ. Amen.

The Reflection   (The Eternal Flame)
"The Father runs before we speak."

The Charge
Receive His embrace today—then extend it to others.

Luke 24:32
"Hearts Burned Within"

The Spark
"Did not our hearts burn within us while he talked to us on the road, while he opened to us the Scriptures?"

The Devotional
The risen Christ walked with disciples unrecognized until their hearts ignited. His presence and His word lit a fire no despair could quench. Revelation often comes not in the spectacular but in the steady unfolding of Scripture.

When Christ opens the Word, hearts burn. His Spirit still kindles the same flame when Scripture is read with Him near. The mark of true encounter is not mere insight but burning hearts.

The Prayer
Adoration: Lord, You are the Living Word who makes Scripture blaze. Confession: Forgive me for reading without seeking Your presence. Petition: Open my eyes to see You in Your Word. Declaration: I declare that my heart will burn as You speak. Amen.

The Reflection   (The Eternal Flame)
"His Word burns when His presence opens it."

The Charge
Open Scripture with Him today—expect fire in your heart.

John 1:14
"Full of Grace and Truth"

The Spark
"And the Word became flesh and dwelt among us, and we have seen his glory, glory as of the only Son from the Father, full of grace and truth."

The Devotional
The eternal Word took on flesh. Glory was no longer distant but dwelling. In Christ, divinity clothed itself with humanity, and truth kissed grace in perfect harmony.

Every other revelation of God pointed forward to this moment: the Word walking among us. Grace without truth collapses into sentiment; truth without grace hardens into law. In Christ, both shine together in fullness.

The Prayer
Adoration: Lord Jesus, You are the Word made flesh, full of grace and truth. Confession: Forgive me for separating what You hold together. Petition: Fill me with both Your grace and Your truth. Declaration: I declare that in Christ I have seen the glory of God. Amen.

The Reflection   (The Eternal Flame)
"Glory is grace and truth in flesh."

The Charge
Walk in both grace and truth today—Christ dwells in you.

John 10:11
"The Good Shepherd"

The Spark
"I am the good shepherd. The good shepherd lays down his life for the sheep."

The Devotional
Shepherds guard, guide, and give—but Jesus goes further. He lays down His life. The cross is not a failure of protection but the fulfillment of it.

The Good Shepherd does not abandon in danger but steps into it, absorbing death to secure life. To belong to Him is to be known, led, and kept at the cost of His blood.

The Prayer
Adoration: Lord, You are the Good Shepherd who gave Your life for me. Confession: Forgive me for wandering from Your voice. Petition: Lead me by Your Spirit into safe pastures. Declaration: I declare that I am kept by the Shepherd's care. Amen.

The Reflection (The Eternal Flame)
"The Shepherd proves His goodness in sacrifice."

The Charge
Follow His voice today—the Shepherd has laid down His life for you.

John 20:16
"Mary"

The Spark
"Jesus said to her, 'Mary.' She turned and said to him in Aramaic, 'Rabboni!' (which means Teacher)."

The Devotional
Mary's grief blinded her until Jesus called her by name. One word— her name— shattered sorrow and revealed resurrection. Christ is not distant; He is personal. His call is intimate, His voice unmistakable.

We, too, are known by name. The risen Lord calls each of us personally, and in that moment, despair turns to recognition, and death yields to life. Resurrection is not abstract—it is relational.

The Prayer
Adoration: Lord, You are the risen Savior who knows me by name. Confession: Forgive me for doubting Your presence in my grief. Petition: Let me hear Your voice calling me again today. Declaration: I declare that I am known and called by name. Amen.

The Reflection   (The Eternal Flame)
"Resurrection is heard when He calls your name."

The Charge
Listen for His voice today—He still calls His own by name.

John 21:17
"Do You Love Me?"

The Spark
"He said to him the third time, 'Simon, son of John, do you love me?' Peter was grieved… and he said to him, 'Lord, you know everything; you know that I love you.' Jesus said to him, 'Feed my sheep.'"

The Devotional
Three denials, three questions, three commissions. Jesus restored Peter not by ignoring his failure but by confronting it with love. Grace does not erase history but rewrites it.

Love for Christ is not sentiment—it is service. To love Him is to feed His sheep, to care for His people. Restoration leads to mission.

The Prayer
Adoration: Lord, You are the restorer of the fallen. Confession: Forgive me for denying You in my words or actions. Petition: Rekindle my love and commission me again. Declaration: I declare that love for Christ will shape my service.
Amen.

The Reflection (The Eternal Flame)
"Love for Him is proven in care for His sheep."

The Charge
Show your love for Christ today by serving His people.

Acts 1:8
"Witnesses to the Ends"

The Spark
"But you will receive power when the Holy Spirit has come upon you, and you will be my witnesses… to the end of the earth."

The Devotional
Jesus tied the mission to the Spirit. Power precedes witness. The Church is not sustained by charisma or strategy but by Spirit-filled testimony.

Witness is not optional; it is identity. To receive the Spirit is to receive commission—to testify in word and life that Christ is Lord, here and to the ends of the earth.

The Prayer
Adoration: Lord, You are the sender of the Spirit and Lord of the harvest. Confession: Forgive me for shrinking back from witness. Petition: Clothe me with power from on high. Declaration: I declare that I am a Spirit-filled witness of Christ. Amen.

The Reflection   (The Eternal Flame)
"The Spirit empowers what Christ commands."

The Charge
Open your mouth today—be His witness where you are.

Romans 8:28
"All Things for Good"

The Spark
"And we know that for those who love God all things work together for good, for those who are called according to his purpose."

The Devotional
Paul does not promise that all things are good, but that God works them for good. Even pain and loss bend under His sovereignty.

This is not naïve optimism but deep assurance. The condition is love and calling—those bound to God by covenant can rest knowing nothing is wasted. Providence redeems even the darkest threads into beauty.

The Prayer
Adoration: Lord, You are the Redeemer of all things. Confession: Forgive me for doubting Your purpose in suffering. Petition: Teach me to trust that You are weaving good from every strand. Declaration: I declare that all things are working together for good. Amen.

The Reflection   (The Eternal Flame)
"God weaves good from every thread."

The Charge
Trust His weaving today—even what seems dark has purpose.

1 Corinthians 1:27
"Foolish to Shame the Wise"

The Spark
"But God chose what is foolish in the world to shame the wise; God chose what is weak in the world to shame the strong."

The Devotional
God overturns human categories. The cross itself—the epitome of weakness— became wisdom and power. He chooses the overlooked and unlikely to display His glory.

This means no one is disqualified by weakness. In fact, weakness becomes the stage for His strength. The world may sneer, but heaven rejoices at such reversals.

The Prayer
Adoration: Lord, You are wisdom higher than human pride. Confession: Forgive me for despising weakness in myself or others. Petition: Use my weakness as a canvas for Your glory. Declaration: I declare that the foolishness of God is wiser than man. Amen.

The Reflection (The Eternal Flame)
"Weakness becomes wisdom when God chooses."

The Charge
Offer your weakness to Him today—watch His glory shine.

2 Corinthians 12:9
"Grace Is Sufficient"

The Spark
"But he said to me, 'My grace is sufficient for you, for my power is made perfect in weakness.' Therefore I will boast all the more gladly of my weaknesses, so that the power of Christ may rest upon me."

The Devotional
Paul pleaded for relief, but God gave something greater: sustaining grace. Weakness was not removed but transformed into the platform for divine power.

Sufficiency is not the absence of weakness but the presence of grace. To boast in weakness is not self-pity but Christ-exaltation—where we lack, His power rests.

The Prayer
Adoration: Lord, Your grace is greater than my weakness. Confession: Forgive me for despising the places where I am weak. Petition: Teach me to boast in my weakness that Christ may be glorified. Declaration: I declare that His grace is sufficient and His power perfected. Amen.

The Reflection (The Eternal Flame)
"Weakness is where grace rests."

The Charge
Lean on His grace today—it is sufficient for you.

Galatians 2:20
"Christ Lives in Me"

The Spark
"I have been crucified with Christ. It is no longer I who live, but Christ who lives in me. And the life I now live in the flesh I live by faith in the Son of God, who loved me and gave himself for me."

The Devotional
Union with Christ is not symbolic—it is reality. The old self was crucified with Him, and the new life is His life in us. Identity is no longer self-defined but Christ- defined.

Faith is not just believing about Christ but living in Him. The life we live is sustained by His love, secured by His sacrifice, and empowered by His presence within.

The Prayer
Adoration: Lord, You are the indwelling Christ, my life and strength. Confession: Forgive me for living as if I were still my own. Petition: Teach me to live daily from union with You. Declaration: I declare that Christ lives in me by faith. Amen.

The Reflection (The Eternal Flame)
"The Christian life is Christ in you."

The Charge
Live today as one crucified with Christ, alive in Him.

Ephesians 3:20
"More Than We Ask"

The Spark
"Now to him who is able to do far more abundantly than all that we ask or think, according to the power at work within us."

The Devotional
Paul lifts our eyes to God's capacity—far beyond imagination or request. His power is not distant but at work within us, multiplying our prayers beyond measure.

Faith does not shrink God to our limits but stretches us to His abundance. He delights to exceed expectation, not occasionally but continually, because His power is inexhaustible.

The Prayer
Adoration: Lord, You are able to do far more than I ask or imagine. Confession: Forgive me for limiting You with small faith. Petition: Expand my vision to pray bold prayers. Declaration: I declare that Your power at work in me exceeds my imagination. Amen.

The Reflection   (The Eternal Flame)
"His power exceeds our prayers."

The Charge
Ask boldly today—He does more than you think.

Philippians 1:6
"He Will Complete It"

The Spark
"And I am sure of this, that he who began a good work in you will bring it to completion at the day of Jesus Christ."

The Devotional
Confidence in the Christian life is not in our ability to finish but in His promise to complete. The God who begins never abandons. What He starts in grace, He finishes in glory.

We stumble, falter, and doubt—but His hand remains steady. The unfinished is not uncertain; it is guaranteed by the faithfulness of Christ

The Prayer
Adoration: Lord, You are faithful from beginning to end. Confession: Forgive me for doubting Your commitment to finish what You start. Petition: Keep me steady until the day of completion. Declaration: I declare that the work begun in me will be completed in Christ. Amen.

The Reflection (The Eternal Flame)
"God finishes what He begins."

The Charge
Rest today in His promise—He will complete it.

Colossians 1:17
"Held Together"

The Spark
"And he is before all things, and in him all things hold together

The Devotional
Christ is not only Creator but Sustainer. Every atom, every star, every heartbea—held by His will. Nothing holds without Him.

When life feels fragmented, this truth steadies us: He holds all things, including us. What seems like chaos is still bound by His sustaining hand.

The Prayer
Adoration: Lord, You are the sustainer of all creation. Confession: Forgive me for believing life rests in my control. Petition: Hold me together when I feel undone. Declaration: I declare that in Christ all things are held together. Amen.

The Reflection (The Eternal Flame)
"Christ holds all things—including you."

The Charge
Trust Him today to hold what feels like it's falling apart.

1 Thessalonians 5:24
"He Will Do It"

The Spark
"He who calls you is faithful; he will surely do it."

The Devotional
Paul roots assurance in God's faithfulness, not our resolve. The One who calls is the One who accomplishes. Sanctification is not self-driven but Spirit-sustained.

God's promises are backed by His character. To doubt His completion is to doubt His faithfulness. He who calls equips; He who begins finishes; He who promises fulfills.

The Prayer
Adoration: Lord, You are faithful and true in all You do. Confession: Forgive me for doubting Your ability to complete what You start. Petition: Strengthen my trust in Your faithful work. Declaration: I declare that He who calls me is faithful. He will do it. Amen.

The Reflection (The Eternal Flame)
"The Caller is the Completer."

The Charge
Lean on His faithfulness today—He will surely do it.

2 Thessalonians 3:3
"The Lord Is Faithful"

The Spark
"But the Lord is faithful. He will establish you and guard you against the evil one."

The Devotional
Paul assures believers that God's faithfulness is their shield. The evil one opposes, but the Lord guards. Faithfulness is not passive—it establishes, strengthens, protects.

We are not left to resist in our own strength. God Himself stands between us and the enemy, securing us in His steadfast faithfulness.

The Prayer
Adoration: Lord, You are my faithful protector. Confession: Forgive me for fearing the enemy more than trusting You. Petition: Establish me in Your truth and guard me from the evil one. Declaration: I declare that the faithful Lord guards and keeps me. Amen.

The Reflection   (The Eternal Flame)
"Faithfulness is God's shield for His people."

The Charge
Walk in confidence today—the faithful Lord guards you.

1 Timothy 6:12
"Fight the Good Fight"

The Spark
"Fight the good fight of the faith. Take hold of the eternal life to which you were called…"

The Devotional
Paul reminds Timothy that faith is not passive—it is a battle. The fight is not against flesh and blood but for faith itself. To fight well is to cling to Christ, refusing to surrender to doubt, sin, or distraction.

Eternal life is not distant—it is the present prize of faith. The good fight is waged with truth as weapon and perseverance as shield. The victory belongs to those who endure.

The Prayer
Adoration: Lord, You are my Captain and my Crown. Confession: Forgive me for laying down my guard in battle. Petition: Strengthen me to fight faithfully today. Declaration: I declare that I will fight the good fight by Your power. Amen.

The Reflection (The Eternal Flame)
"Faith is a fight worth every wound."

The Charge
Hold fast to Christ—fight well today.

2 Timothy 1:7
"Spirit of Power"

The Spark
"For God gave us a spirit not of fear but of power and love and self-control."

The Devotional
Fear is not from God. His Spirit is not timid but triumphant—marked by power, love, and discipline. Fear enslaves, but the Spirit liberates.

Power without love destroys; love without power weakens; both require discipline. The Spirit unites all three, shaping us to live courageously, compassionately, and wisely.

The Prayer
Adoration: Lord, You are power, love, and wisdom. Confession: Forgive me for yielding to fear instead of faith. Petition: Fill me with Your Spirit of courage and love. Declaration: I declare that fear has no place—the Spirit empowers me. Amen.

The Reflection   (The Eternal Flame)
"The Spirit conquers fear with power, love, and wisdom."

The Charge
Walk today in Spirit-given courage.

Titus 3:5
"Not by Works"

The Spark
"He saved us, not because of works done by us in righteousness, but according to his own mercy…"

The Devotional
Salvation rests not on works but mercy. Even our best efforts cannot purchase grace. God saves by His mercy, not our merit.

This humbles pride and lifts despair. For the self-righteous, it strips boasting. For the broken, it offers hope. Mercy is the ground on which all stand.

The Prayer
Adoration: Lord, You are merciful and mighty to save. Confession: Forgive me for trusting my works over Your mercy. Petition: Root me deeper in the assurance of Your grace. Declaration: I declare that salvation is by mercy alone. Amen.

The Reflection   (The Eternal Flame)
"Grace saves where works fail."

The Charge
Rest in His mercy today—it is enough.

Philemon 1:6
"Faith Becomes Effective"

The Spark
"I pray that the sharing of your faith may become effective for the full knowledge of every good thing that is in us for the sake of Christ."

The Devotional
Paul prays that faith would overflow in witness. Faith is not static—it becomes effective as it is shared. In giving, we gain; in testifying, we deepen our knowledge of Christ's riches.

The gospel is not meant to be hoarded but spread. Faith is strengthened in the telling. What we share multiplies within.

The Prayer
Adoration: Lord, You are the giver of every good thing. Confession: Forgive me for silencing my faith. Petition: Make my witness effective for Your glory.

Declaration: I declare that shared faith multiplies joy in Christ. Amen.

The Reflection (The Eternal Flame)
"Faith grows stronger when it is shared."

The Charge
Share your faith today—it will grow as you give it away.

Hebrews 4:12
"Sharper Than a Sword"

The Spark
"For the word of God is living and active, sharper than any two-edged sword, piercing to the division of soul and of spirit... discerning the thoughts and intentions of the heart."

The Devotional
Scripture is not static text but living power. It pierces deeper than any human word, cutting through appearances to the very core of who we are.

The Word reveals, divides, convicts, and heals. Its sharpness is not cruelty but clarity—exposing what is hidden so truth may reign. To handle the Word is to encounter God Himself.

The Prayer
Adoration: Lord, Your Word is alive and sharp with truth. Confession: Forgive me for dulling my heart against its edge. Petition: Let Your Word cut away what hinders and heal what is broken. Declaration: I declare that the living Word discerns and transforms me. Amen.

The Reflection (The Eternal Flame)
"The Word cuts to heal."

The Charge
Let Scripture pierce you today—it cuts to make whole.

James 1:5
"Ask for Wisdom"

The Spark
"If any of you lacks wisdom, let him ask God, who gives generously to all without reproach, and it will be given him."

The Devotional
God does not shame those who lack; He invites them to ask. Wisdom is His gift, given generously to the humble. The only condition is faith to receive.

True wisdom is not human cleverness but divine perspective. It steadies us in trial, guides us in decisions, and keeps us from folly.

The Prayer
Adoration: Lord, You are the source of all wisdom. Confession: Forgive me for seeking human counsel above Yours. Petition: Grant me wisdom generously as I ask in faith. Declaration: I declare that the God of wisdom gives without reproach. Amen.

The Reflection (The Eternal Flame)
"Wisdom flows to those who ask in faith."

The Charge
Ask Him boldly today—He delights to give wisdom.

1 Peter 5:7
"Cast Your Cares"

The Spark
"Casting all your anxieties on him, because he cares for you."

The Devotional
Anxieties weigh heavy, but Peter invites us to throw them—forcefully and fully— onto Christ. The reason is not duty but care. The Almighty does not despise our burdens; He welcomes them.

To cast is to release. To cling is to remain crushed. His care is not abstract—it is personal, attentive, constant. We are never designed to carry what only Christ can bear.

The Prayer
Adoration: Lord, You are the caring Shepherd of my soul. Confession: Forgive me for clutching anxieties instead of casting them. Petition: Teach me to release every care into Your hands. Declaration: I declare that Christ cares for me and carries my burdens. Amen.

The Reflection (The Eternal Flame)
"His care is greater than your cares."

The Charge
Cast every anxiety today—don't carry what He has claimed.

1 John 4:18
"Perfect Love Casts Out Fear"

The Spark
"There is no fear in love, but perfect love casts out fear. For fear has to do with punishment, and whoever fears has not been perfected in love."

The Devotional
Fear thrives where love is doubted. God's perfect love does not merely comfort— it expels fear. Fear cannot coexist with the assurance of being fully loved.

The cross proves love perfected. Punishment is borne by Christ; judgment no longer threatens. To abide in love is to live fearless, not because life is safe, but because love is sure.

The Prayer
Adoration: Lord, You are perfect love revealed in Christ. Confession: Forgive me for living as if I were unloved. Petition: Perfect me in Your love until fear has no hold. Declaration: I declare that perfect love casts out all fear. Amen.

The Reflection (The Eternal Flame)
"Fear flees where love reigns."

The Charge

Rest today in perfect love—fear has no place

2 John 1:6 & 3 John 1:4
"Walk in the Truth"

The Spark

"And this is love, that we walk according to his commandments" 2 John 1 6 .
"I have no greater joy than to hear that my children are walking in the truth" 3 John 1 4 .

The Devotional

Both of John's brief letters strike a common theme: truth must be walked, not just spoken. Love expresses itself in obedience, and joy is found when the next generation continues in the truth.

2 John reminds us that love and truth are inseparable—obedience is love in action. 3 John reveals the heart of a shepherd, rejoicing when disciples live what they profess. Together, they teach that truth is not an idea but a path, and love is the step that walks it.

The Prayer

Adoration: Lord, You are the Truth and the One who leads in love. Confession: Forgive me for separating love from obedience. Petition: Help me walk daily in truth and love. Declaration: I declare that love obeys, and truth is lived. Amen.

The Reflection (The Eternal Flame)

"Truth is proven in the walk, and love is seen in obedience.

The Charge
Walk today in both truth and love—this is joy to God's heart.

Revelation 21:5 "All Things New"

The Spark
"And he who was seated on the throne said, 'Behold, I am making all things new.'"

The Devotional
The Bible ends with renewal, not ruin. The enthroned Christ declares the future certain: all things made new. Creation groans now, but restoration is coming.

This is not repair but recreation. The former things—pain, tears, death—pass away. The final word is not brokenness but newness, secured by the risen Lamb who reigns forever.

The Prayer
Adoration: Lord, You are the Alpha and Omega, making all things new. Confession: Forgive me for despairing as if renewal will not come. Petition: Fix my eyes on the hope of Your new creation. Declaration: I declare that the One on the throne makes all things new. Amen.

The Reflection (The Eternal Flame)
"The final word is newness, not ruin."

The Charge
Live today in hope—new creation is coming.

Epilogue

The fire has not ended—it has only begun.

From Genesis to Revelation, the Word of God reveals a single flame: holy, relentless, and eternal. These devotionals were never meant to be consumed and set aside, but carried forward as embers into daily life.

The God who spoke light into darkness still speaks. The Spirit who breathed on prophets still breathes. The Christ who walked among us still reigns, and His kingdom still burns brighter than the night.

So let these sparks not remain on the page. Let them kindle in your heart, ignite in your prayers, and blaze in your witness. The world does not need more noise; it needs fire.

Take this flame into your home, your work, your community. Let your life become a living torch—burning with truth, saturated with love, unstoppable in hope.

For the God who makes all things new has already set eternity alight within you. Carry the fire.

—Lev Montgomery

Flashes of Fire: 66 Devotionals and Prayers Across Scripture

From the opening command of "Light be" in Genesis to the triumphant promise "Behold, I am making all things new" in Revelation, Scripture burns with divine fire.

In Flashes of Fire, Lev Montgomery guides you through all sixty-six books of the Bible with lightning devotionals and prayers designed to strike quickly but burn deeply. Each entry includes:

A Scripture Spark drawn from the heart of the text.

A devotional meditation—brief yet profound, crafted to ignite faith.

A prayer sequence to anchor you in worship, confession, petition, and declaration.

A one-line reflection—a lasting ember to carry into your day.

These are not long readings but luminous bursts of truth—crafted for seekers, leaders, and believers who long to walk in the fire of God's Word.

Whether read daily or as a journey through the whole canon, this book invites you to encounter the living God, one spark at a time.

The Word is fire. Let it burn in you.

About the Author

Lev Montgomery is a faith-driven writer, speaker, and visionary, known for his luminous voice and ability to blend biblical depth with prophetic clarity. Through his work with Pen & Press Publishing LLC, Lev equips readers and leaders to live as torchbearers of truth in a darkening world.

His calling is simple yet consuming: to awaken hearts to the fire of God's Word and to cultivate a generation marked by devotion, prayer, and holy courage.

When not writing, Lev invests in ministry, mentorship, and creative expression that bridges faith, culture, and community.

This is his debut devotional book—crafted not as mere commentary but as an invitation: to step into Scripture's flame and carry it into the world.

Notes

www.ingramcontent.com/pod-product-compliance
Lightning Source LLC
Chambersburg PA
CBHW050910160426
43194CB00011B/2350